RED-EARED SLIDERS

Comprehensive Guide To Turtles Care, Habitat, Distribution, Characteristics, Behavior, Temperament, Housing, Enclosure, Tank, Lighting, Heating, Health, Breeding, And Enrichment

Ethan Harry

Table of Contents

CHAPTER ONE

INTRODUCTION TO RED-EARED SLIDERS

Overview Of Red-Eared Sliders

Red-Eared Sliders (Trachemys scripta elegans) are among the most popular pet turtles worldwide. Recognized for the distinctive red markings around their ears, these turtles are a subspecies of pond sliders. Native to the southern United States and northern Mexico, they have garnered widespread popularity due to their appealing appearance and relatively straightforward care requirements.

These turtles are semi-aquatic, meaning they thrive both in water and on land. In their natural habitat, Red-Eared Sliders are commonly found in freshwater environments such as ponds, lakes, and rivers. They are particularly fond of basking, often seen soaking up the sun on logs or rocks near the water's edge. This behavior is not just a leisurely activity; it is essential for their health as it helps regulate their body temperature and supports their metabolic processes.

Red-Eared Sliders are omnivorous, with a diet that includes both plant and animal matter. In the wild, they consume a variety of foods, including aquatic plants, small fish, insects, and even carrion. This diverse diet ensures they receive a balanced intake of nutrients necessary for their growth and health. In captivity, their diet is typically more controlled and can consist of commercial turtle pellets designed to provide a comprehensive nutritional profile. Additionally, it is important to supplement their diet with fresh vegetables such as lettuce, carrots, and aquatic plants.

Occasional protein sources like fish, insects, or cooked chicken can also be included to mimic their natural dietary habits.

Caring for Red-Eared Sliders involves creating an environment that closely replicates their natural habitat. This includes providing a spacious aquarium with both water for swimming and a dry area for basking. The water should be kept clean and at an appropriate temperature, typically between 75 and 85 degrees Fahrenheit, to maintain their health. A water filtration system is crucial to keep the environment hygienic and free of harmful bacteria.

Basking areas should be equipped with a heat lamp to ensure the turtles can properly thermoregulate. Additionally, UVB lighting is essential for their shell and bone health, as it enables them to synthesize vitamin D3, crucial for calcium absorption. Without adequate UVB exposure, Red-Eared Sliders can develop serious health issues, including metabolic bone disease.

Behaviorally, these turtles are active and curious, often engaging with their environment and exploring their surroundings. They can live for several decades, with some individuals reaching over 30 years of age when properly cared for. This long lifespan makes them a significant commitment for potential pet owners.

Natural Habitat And Distribution

Red-Eared Sliders thrive in specific aquatic environments that cater to their unique physiological and behavioral needs. In their natural habitat, these turtles are commonly found in slow-moving bodies of water such as ponds, lakes, marshes, and rivers. These environments typically feature soft, muddy bottoms which are ideal for burrowing and foraging. Additionally, the presence of abundant aquatic vegetation in these areas is crucial, as it provides food, shelter, and hiding spots from predators.

One of the distinctive behaviors of Red-Eared Sliders is their penchant for basking. They seek out sunny basking spots, such as logs, rocks, or the banks of water bodies, where they can climb out of the water and absorb sunlight. Basking is a vital activity for these turtles as it allows them to regulate their body temperature, which is essential for metabolic processes. The warmth from the sun also aids in digestion and is crucial for maintaining shell health, preventing fungal and bacterial infections. Without regular basking, these turtles can suffer from a range of health issues, including metabolic bone disease and shell rot.

Geographically, Red-Eared Sliders are native to the southeastern United States. Their natural range extends from the Gulf Coast states, such as Texas and Louisiana, through to Florida and up the Atlantic coast to Virginia. They are also found in parts of Mexico. In these regions, the climate and water conditions are well-suited to their needs, with ample warmth and appropriate humidity levels.

However, the popularity of Red-Eared Sliders as pets has led to their introduction in various other parts of the world. Often, pet owners release these turtles into the wild when they can no longer care for them. As a result, Red-Eared Sliders have established populations in many non-native regions, including Europe, Asia, and Australia. In these new environments, they can become highly invasive. Their adaptability allows them to thrive, sometimes to the detriment of local ecosystems. They often outcompete native turtle species for resources such as food and basking sites, which can lead to declines in indigenous populations. Additionally, their presence can disrupt local aquatic vegetation and invertebrate communities.

The widespread distribution of Red-Eared Sliders highlights the impact of human activity on wildlife. While they are a resilient and adaptable species, their success in non-native habitats raises important conservation and ecological questions. Efforts to manage their populations in these areas are essential to protect native species and maintain ecological balance.

Physical Characteristics And Identification

Red-Eared Sliders are medium-sized turtles, with adults typically measuring between 6 to 12 inches in length. Their distinctive appearance makes them relatively easy to identify. The most notable feature is the red stripe behind each eye, which is the origin of their common name. Their shells are usually green with yellow markings, and their skin is green with yellow stripes, creating a striking contrast that makes them easily recognizable.

Juvenile Red-Eared Sliders are particularly vibrant, boasting bright green shells and clear red markings that are more pronounced than in adults. As they age, their colors may become duller, and algae can grow on their shells, giving them a more muted appearance. This algae growth is a natural occurrence and does not harm the turtles but rather provides some camouflage in their aquatic environments. The undersides of their shells, known as plastrons, are typically yellow with dark markings, which can also aid in identification.

In terms of sexual dimorphism, males and females can be distinguished by several physical traits. Males generally have longer claws on their front feet, which they use during courtship displays to attract females. These claws are particularly useful in the water, where males will flutter them around the females' faces as part of their mating ritual. Additionally, males have longer, thicker tails compared to females. The cloaca of the male is located further down the tail, which is another distinguishing feature.

Females, on the other hand, usually grow larger than males. While males reach a maximum length of around 10 inches, females can grow up to 12 inches or more. Female Red-Eared Sliders also have shorter claws and tails compared to their male counterparts. The shorter claws are a noticeable feature and make it easier to differentiate between the sexes.

The coloration and pattern of Red-Eared Sliders can also vary based on their habitat and health. Those living in cleaner water tend to have brighter and clearer markings, while those in murkier or algae-rich environments may appear duller due to the buildup on their shells. Healthy Red-Eared Sliders typically have smooth, hard shells without any signs of pitting or soft spots, which can indicate shell rot or other health issues.

Behavior And Temperament

Red-Eared Sliders are known for their active and curious nature. In the wild, they can often be seen basking in groups on logs or rocks, a behavior that is essential for thermoregulation and vitamin D synthesis. These turtles are highly alert and will quickly slide into the water if they sense danger, a natural defense mechanism to avoid predators. Their excellent swimming abilities allow them to spend a significant amount of time foraging for food underwater, where they can remain submerged for extended periods due to their efficient respiratory systems.

In captivity, Red-Eared Sliders can exhibit a range of interactive behaviors with their owners. They often swim to the side of the tank when someone approaches, especially if they associate the person with feeding time. This anticipation is a sign of their intelligence and adaptability to routine. However, they can also be quite skittish and may retreat quickly if startled by sudden movements or loud noises.

Red-Eared Sliders are generally solitary animals and do not require the company of other turtles to thrive. In fact, housing multiple Red-Eared Sliders together can sometimes lead to aggression, particularly among males or during the mating season. Aggressive interactions can result in stress and injury, so if you choose to keep more than one turtle, it is essential to provide ample space and numerous hiding spots to reduce territorial disputes and stress. A large tank with separate basking areas can help mitigate these issues.

Despite their hardy nature, Red-Eared Sliders have specific care requirements that must be met to ensure their health and well-being. Proper housing is crucial, including a clean tank equipped with a good filtration system to maintain water quality. They need a basking area with appropriate UVB lighting to support their metabolic processes and prevent shell deformities. The basking spot should be easily accessible and maintained at a temperature that promotes healthy thermoregulation.

Diet is another critical aspect of their care. Red-Eared Sliders are omnivorous, requiring a varied diet that includes both animal proteins and plant matter. Offering a mix of commercial turtle pellets, live or frozen prey, and fresh vegetables ensures they receive a balanced diet rich in essential nutrients. Regular dietary variation can also stimulate their natural foraging behaviors and keep them engaged.

CHAPTER TWO

HOUSING AND ENCLOSURES

Tank Size And Setup

When creating a suitable home for your red-eared slider, selecting the right tank is paramount. The general guideline is to provide a minimum of 10 gallons of water for every inch of your turtle's shell length. For example, if your turtle measures 4 inches, you will need at least a 40-gallon tank. However, opting for a larger tank is always preferable, as it promotes a healthier environment and allows your turtle to exhibit more natural behaviors.

The tank setup should include both a water area and a dry basking area. The water section needs to be deep enough to enable the turtle to swim comfortably and exercise its natural behaviors. Ideally, the water should allow the turtle to swim freely, which helps maintain its physical health and well-being. The depth should be sufficient for the turtle to fully submerge and swim around, but also shallow enough in some parts to let the turtle rest its feet on the bottom. This variety in depth ensures that the turtle can choose its preferred swimming and resting conditions.

In addition to the water area, a basking area is essential. This dry space allows the turtle to climb out of the water, dry off, and absorb heat and ultraviolet light, which are crucial for its health. The basking area can be created using a floating platform or a pile of rocks that extend above the water surface. The floating platform can be attached to the tank wall or free-floating, providing easy access for the turtle. Rocks should be securely piled to prevent them from shifting and potentially injuring the turtle. The basking spot must be accessible and stable, offering a safe place for the turtle to relax and thermoregulate.

To further enhance the tank setup, ensure the water is kept clean and at the appropriate temperature. Installing a good filtration system is vital for maintaining water quality, reducing the risk of disease, and ensuring the overall health of your turtle. Water heaters may also be necessary to maintain a stable temperature, mimicking the turtle's natural habitat.

Lighting is another critical component of the tank setup. UVB lighting is essential for the turtle's shell and bone health, aiding in the synthesis of vitamin D3, which is necessary for calcium absorption. Position the UVB light above the basking area to maximize its benefits, and ensure it is on for 10-12 hours a day to mimic natural sunlight.

Filtration And Water Quality

Maintaining clean water is crucial for the health of your red-eared slider, as water quality directly impacts their well-being. An effective filtration system is essential for keeping the water clean by removing debris, waste, and harmful chemicals. Among the various types of filters available, canister filters are highly recommended for turtle tanks. They are known for their power and efficiency in handling large amounts of waste, making them an excellent choice for maintaining a healthy aquatic environment for your red-eared slider.

Canister filters work by drawing water from the tank into an external container where it passes through multiple stages of filtration. These stages typically include mechanical filtration, which removes solid waste; biological filtration, which promotes beneficial bacteria that break down harmful substances; and chemical filtration, which removes toxins and impurities. The clean water is then returned to the tank, ensuring a continuous cycle of filtration that keeps the water clean and safe for your turtle.

In addition to having a good filtration system, it's essential to regularly monitor the water quality in your turtle tank. Checking the levels of ammonia, nitrite, and nitrate is crucial because high concentrations of these substances can be harmful to your red-eared slider. Ammonia is produced from waste and uneaten food and is toxic to turtles at high levels. Nitrite, a byproduct of ammonia breakdown, is also harmful, while nitrate, the final product of the nitrogen cycle, is less toxic but still needs to be kept under control.

To monitor these levels, use a water testing kit weekly. This kit will help you identify any imbalances in the water chemistry that could potentially harm your turtle. If you detect high levels of ammonia, nitrite, or nitrate, it's essential to take corrective measures promptly. One effective way to maintain good water quality is through regular partial water changes. Replacing about 25-50% of the water every week helps dilute any accumulated toxins and keeps the environment healthy for your red-eared slider.

When performing water changes, always use dechlorinated water. Tap water contains chlorine and other chemicals that can be harmful to your turtle, so it's crucial to treat the water before adding it to the tank. Dechlorination can be done using water conditioners available at pet stores, which neutralize harmful chemicals and make the water safe for your turtle.

Lighting And Heating Requirements

Proper lighting and heating are crucial for the health and well-being of red-eared sliders. These aquatic turtles require both UVB lighting and an appropriate heat source to thrive. Understanding and implementing the correct lighting and heating setup can prevent several health issues and ensure that your red-eared slider leads a healthy and active life.

UVB lighting is essential for red-eared sliders because it facilitates the production of vitamin D3. This vitamin is critical for calcium absorption, which, in turn, is vital for the development and maintenance of healthy bones. Without sufficient UVB exposure, red-eared sliders can suffer from metabolic bone disease, a condition that can cause severe deformities and other health problems. To provide adequate UVB light, use a bulb specifically designed for reptiles. These bulbs emit the necessary wavelengths of UVB light that turtles need. Position the UVB bulb over the basking area so that your turtle can easily bask under it. It's important to replace UVB bulbs every six months, as their effectiveness diminishes over time even if they still produce visible light.

In addition to UVB lighting, red-eared sliders also require a heat source. The basking area temperature should be maintained between 85-90°F (29-32°C). This can be achieved by using a heat lamp placed directly above the basking spot. The heat lamp should be positioned in a way that allows the turtle to move closer or farther away to regulate its body temperature. This thermoregulation is crucial for their metabolic processes and overall health.

The water temperature in the enclosure is just as important as the basking temperature. Red-eared sliders are ectothermic, meaning they rely on external heat sources to regulate their body temperature. The water should be kept at a consistent temperature between 75-80°F (24-27°C). Using an aquarium heater is the best way to maintain this temperature range. It's essential to choose a reliable heater with a thermostat to ensure the water temperature remains stable. Regularly check the heater to make sure it is functioning correctly.

To monitor the temperatures accurately, place thermometers both in the water and in the basking area. Digital thermometers are often more precise and easier to read than analog ones. Regular monitoring will help you ensure that the environment remains within the optimal temperature ranges, promoting the health and well-being of your red-eared slider.

Substrate And Decorations

Selecting the appropriate substrate for your turtle tank is essential for maintaining your pet's health and the cleanliness of the habitat. It's crucial to avoid using small gravel or pebbles as a substrate. Turtles are curious creatures and may inadvertently ingest small particles while exploring or feeding, which can lead to severe health complications such as intestinal blockages or impactions. These conditions are not only painful for the turtle but can also be life-threatening, requiring immediate veterinary attention.

Instead of small gravel, opt for larger river rocks that are too big for your turtle to swallow. River rocks provide a natural look and are easy to clean. Another option is to leave the tank bottom bare. A bare-bottom tank is simpler to maintain and allows for easier waste removal, helping to keep the water clean and reducing the risk of bacterial buildup. Additionally, a bare-bottom tank can be beneficial for monitoring your turtle's health, as it makes it easier to spot any abnormal droppings or debris.

Decorations play a significant role in enriching your turtle's environment, providing mental stimulation, and encouraging natural behaviors. Hiding spots are particularly important as they offer your turtle a sense of security. These can be created using commercially available caves, PVC pipes, or even custom-made structures. Ensure that any hiding spots are appropriately sized for your turtle to enter and exit comfortably, and that they do not have any sharp edges that could cause injury.

Adding live or artificial plants to the tank can enhance its aesthetic appeal and create a more naturalistic environment. Live plants can help improve water quality by absorbing nitrates, but it's important to choose species that are safe for turtles. Some aquatic plants like anacharis, java fern, and hornwort are generally safe options. However, be prepared for the possibility that your turtle may eat or uproot live plants. To prevent this, you can anchor plants securely or place them in pots.

Artificial plants are a durable alternative that can provide the same visual benefits without the risk of being eaten or uprooted. When selecting artificial plants, ensure they are made from non-toxic materials and free from any small parts that could be ingested.

Outdoor Enclosures

If you live in a suitable climate, setting up an outdoor enclosure for your red-eared slider can be a fantastic option. An outdoor pond offers a more natural environment and provides ample space for the turtle to swim, explore, and engage in natural behaviors. However, there are several important factors to consider to ensure the safety and well-being of your turtle.

First, the pond must be secure. Install sturdy walls or a fence around the enclosure to prevent the turtle from escaping and to protect it from potential predators. The fence should be buried several inches into the ground to prevent the turtle from digging its way out. Additionally, make sure there are no gaps or spaces that the turtle could squeeze through.

The outdoor enclosure should mimic the indoor tank setup, including both water and land areas. The water portion of the pond should be deep enough for the turtle to swim freely but also include shallow areas where the turtle can rest and easily access the land. It's crucial to provide basking spots that allow the turtle to bask in natural sunlight, which is an excellent source of UVB rays necessary for their health. However, it's equally important to provide shaded areas where the turtle can retreat to avoid overheating. Large rocks, logs, or plants can offer these shaded spots. Regular maintenance of the outdoor pond is essential. Water quality should be monitored closely, just as you would with an indoor tank. This includes checking for appropriate pH levels, cleanliness, and ensuring the water is free from harmful chemicals. Installing a filtration system can help maintain clean water, but regular water changes may still be necessary.

Debris such as leaves and twigs should be removed promptly to prevent water contamination.

Temperature control is another critical aspect. While natural sunlight can help maintain the water temperature, you may need to use a pond heater in cooler climates to ensure the water remains at a comfortable temperature for your turtle. During extreme weather conditions, such as very hot or cold temperatures, you may need to move your turtle indoors temporarily to prevent stress or health issues.

CHAPTER THREE

DIET AND NUTRITION

Basic Dietary Needs

Red-Eared Sliders are fascinating omnivores, meaning they consume both plant and animal matter. In their natural habitats, these turtles have a diverse diet that includes aquatic plants, insects, small fish, and occasionally carrion. For pet Red-Eared Sliders, it's crucial to replicate this diet as closely as possible to ensure they receive all the essential nutrients required for their health and well-being.

Protein

Protein is a vital component of a Red-Eared Slider's diet, particularly for young turtles. Hatchlings and juveniles require a higher protein intake to support their rapid growth and development. In captivity, this protein can be provided through a variety of sources. Insects such as crickets and mealworms are excellent choices, offering a natural and enriching food option. Small fish can also be included, mimicking the types of prey they would encounter in the wild. Additionally, commercially available turtle pellets that are high in protein content can be a convenient and balanced option for providing the necessary nutrients.

As Red-Eared Sliders mature, their dietary needs shift, and their requirement for protein decreases. Adult sliders benefit from a more balanced diet with a greater emphasis on plant matter. However, it's still important to include protein sources in their diet, albeit in smaller quantities than for juveniles.

Vegetables

Vegetables play a crucial role in the diet of adult Red-Eared Sliders. Leafy greens such as kale, collard greens, and dandelion greens are particularly beneficial. These greens are rich in vitamins and minerals, supporting the overall health of the turtle. Other vegetables that can be included in their diet are squash, carrots, and bell peppers. These vegetables not only provide essential nutrients but also add variety to their diet, which can help stimulate their appetite and interest in feeding.

Fruits

While fruits should not make up a significant portion of a Red-Eared Slider's diet due to their high sugar content, they can be offered occasionally as a treat. Suitable fruits include apples, berries, and melons. These fruits can provide a source of hydration and additional vitamins, but they should be given sparingly to avoid any potential health issues related to excessive sugar intake.

Commercial Foods Vs. Natural Diet

Commercial turtle foods offer convenience and are designed to meet the nutritional needs of Red-Eared Sliders. These pellets can serve as a primary component of your turtle's diet, providing a balanced mix of proteins, vitamins, and minerals essential for their health. However, it is not advisable to rely solely on commercial food.

Pros of Commercial Foods

Convenience: One of the main advantages of commercial turtle food is its ease of use. These pellets are easy to store and feed, making them a hassle-free option for turtle owners. You can simply measure the appropriate amount and offer it to your turtle without any preparation.

Nutritionally balanced: Commercial foods are formulated to meet the dietary requirements of turtles. They contain a mix of proteins, vitamins, and minerals that support overall health, growth, and development. This ensures that your turtle receives a balanced diet without the need for supplementation.

Long shelf life: Another benefit of commercial turtle food is its long shelf life. Unlike fresh foods, which can spoil quickly, commercial pellets can be stored for extended periods without losing their nutritional value. This reduces the risk of spoilage and wastage, providing a reliable food source for your turtle.

Cons of Commercial Foods

Lack of variety: One major drawback of feeding only commercial pellets is the lack of variety in your turtle's diet. Consuming the same food every day can become monotonous for turtles, potentially leading to decreased appetite and nutritional deficiencies. Turtles, like other animals, benefit from a varied diet that includes different textures and flavors.

Potential additives: Some commercial turtle foods may contain preservatives and artificial ingredients to extend shelf life and enhance palatability. These additives can be detrimental to your turtle's health in the long run. It is essential to choose high-quality commercial foods without harmful additives and to read ingredient labels carefully.

Incorporating natural foods, such as fresh vegetables and live prey, ensures a more diverse and enriching diet for your Red-Eared Slider. Fresh vegetables like leafy greens, carrots, and bell peppers provide essential vitamins and minerals that may not be present in commercial pellets. Live prey, such as insects and small fish, offer protein and stimulate natural hunting behaviors.

A balanced diet should include a mix of commercial pellets and natural foods. This approach not only meets the nutritional needs of your turtle but also promotes mental stimulation and natural foraging behaviors. By offering a variety of foods, you can keep your turtle healthy, engaged, and satisfied with its diet.

Feeding Schedule And Portion Sizes

Establishing a regular feeding schedule is crucial for maintaining the health and well-being of your Red-Eared Slider. The frequency and portion sizes of their meals will vary depending on the turtle's age and size. Understanding these differences and adhering to appropriate feeding practices can prevent health issues related to both overfeeding and underfeeding.

Juvenile Turtles (up to 1 year old)

Juvenile Red-Eared Sliders require daily feeding to support their rapid growth and high energy needs. For these young turtles, it is recommended to provide food once a day. The portion size should be roughly equivalent to the size of the turtle's head, excluding the neck. This guideline helps ensure that they receive adequate nutrition without the risk of overfeeding. Juvenile turtles are particularly active and need a diet that supports their development, which includes a mix of proteins and vegetables. Observing their growth and adjusting the portion sizes accordingly is important to avoid potential health problems such as obesity or malnutrition.

Adult Turtles (over 1 year old)

As Red-Eared Sliders mature and their growth rate slows, their feeding frequency and portion sizes should be adjusted. Adult turtles should be fed every other day, with the portion size remaining approximately the size of the turtle's head. This adjustment helps maintain a healthy weight and prevents overfeeding, which can lead to obesity and related health issues. Adult turtles still require a balanced diet, but the reduced feeding frequency reflects their decreased metabolic rate compared to juveniles. Including a variety of foods in their diet, such as leafy greens, aquatic plants, and occasional protein sources, can help meet their nutritional needs.

Monitoring and Adjustments

Regularly observing your Red-Eared Slider's behavior and body condition is essential in maintaining their health. Turtles that are overfed may exhibit signs of obesity, such as a noticeable layer of fat around their limbs or difficulty retracting into their shells. Conversely, underfed turtles may appear lethargic, have a prominent shell, or show signs of malnutrition, such as a weakened immune system or poor growth. If you notice any of these signs, adjusting the portion sizes and frequency of feedings can help correct the imbalance.

Supplements And Treats

Ensuring that your Red-Eared Slider receives all the necessary nutrients is vital for their health and well-being. While a balanced diet primarily composed of commercial turtle pellets, vegetables, and occasional fruits is essential, supplements can help fill in any nutritional gaps. Here's a closer look at the importance of supplements and the types of treats that can be beneficial for your Red-Eared Slider.

Calcium Supplements

Calcium is crucial for the healthy development of your turtle's shell and bones. Without adequate calcium, Red-Eared Sliders can develop metabolic bone disease, which can be fatal. One of the most effective ways to provide calcium is through cuttlebone. Not only is cuttlebone a rich source of calcium, but it also serves the dual purpose of aiding in the maintenance of beak health. The act of gnawing on cuttlebone encourages natural wear and helps prevent the beak from becoming overgrown, which can interfere with feeding and cause discomfort.

Vitamin Supplements

In addition to calcium, vitamins are essential to the overall health of Red-Eared Sliders. Vitamin D3 is particularly important, as it helps in the absorption of calcium. Red-Eared Sliders naturally synthesize vitamin D3 when exposed to sunlight. However, if your turtle does not receive sufficient sunlight, you may need to provide vitamin D3 supplements. These can come in liquid or powder form and should be used sparingly and according to veterinary advice, as excessive vitamin D3 can lead to toxicity.

Treats

While supplements ensure that your Red-Eared Slider receives the necessary nutrients, treats can provide mental stimulation and enrichment. However, it is important to remember that treats should be given sparingly and should not replace regular, balanced meals.

Live Prey

Live prey, such as small fish or earthworms, can be excellent treats for Red-Eared Sliders. These treats not only provide nutritional benefits but also stimulate natural hunting behaviors. The act of hunting live prey can keep your turtle mentally engaged and physically active.

Fruits

Fruits can also be given as occasional treats due to their high sugar content. Options like berries, apples, and melons can be offered in small amounts. However, fruits should not make up a significant portion of the diet, as excessive sugar can lead to health issues.

Human Food

Avoid feeding your Red-Eared Slider human food, particularly those high in fat, salt, or sugar. These foods can cause serious health problems and do not provide the necessary nutrients that your turtle needs.

CHAPTER FOUR

HEALTH AND WELLNESS

Common Health Issues

Red-Eared Sliders, like all pets, are susceptible to a variety of health issues that can impact their well-being if not properly managed. Some of the most common health problems these turtles face include shell rot, respiratory infections, parasites, vitamin A deficiency, and metabolic bone disease.

Shell rot is a prevalent condition among Red-Eared Sliders, characterized by soft, discolored patches on the shell. This condition typically arises when the turtle's shell is damaged, often due to improper habitat conditions or injuries, allowing bacteria or fungi to invade and cause infection. If left untreated, shell rot can lead to severe infections that may compromise the turtle's overall health. Early detection and prompt treatment are essential, usually involving cleaning the affected area and applying topical antibiotics.

Respiratory infections are another common health issue in Red-Eared Sliders. These infections can be identified by symptoms such as wheezing, mucus around the nose, and difficulty breathing. They are often caused by poor water quality, inadequate basking areas, or exposure to cold temperatures. Respiratory infections can quickly become severe, potentially leading to pneumonia. Therefore, maintaining optimal habitat conditions, including clean water, proper basking temperatures, and adequate UVB lighting, is crucial for prevention. If a respiratory infection is suspected, veterinary care is necessary to provide appropriate antibiotics and supportive care.

Parasites, both internal and external, can also affect Red-Eared Sliders. Internal parasites, like worms, can cause weight loss, lethargy, and digestive issues. External parasites, such as leeches, can be seen attached to the turtle's skin or shell. Regular health checks and fecal exams by a veterinarian can help detect and treat parasitic infestations. Treatment typically involves antiparasitic medications and maintaining a clean and hygienic environment to prevent re-infestation.

Vitamin A deficiency is a nutritional issue that can lead to several health problems in Red-Eared Sliders, including swollen eyes, respiratory issues, and a weakened immune system. This deficiency is often caused by a diet lacking in variety and essential nutrients. Providing a balanced diet that includes leafy greens, vegetables, and vitamin A-rich foods like carrots and sweet potatoes can help prevent this deficiency. In severe cases, vitamin A supplements may be necessary under veterinary guidance.

Metabolic bone disease (MBD) is a significant health concern for Red-Eared Sliders, resulting from a lack of calcium or vitamin D3. MBD leads to weak, deformed bones and shells, making the turtle more susceptible to fractures and other injuries. Ensuring the turtle receives a diet rich in calcium, along with proper UVB lighting to facilitate vitamin D3 synthesis, is crucial for preventing MBD. Supplements and dietary adjustments may be required for turtles diagnosed with this condition, along with veterinary care to manage and treat the disease.

Signs Of Illness And Disease

Early detection of illness in your Red-Eared Slider is crucial for its well-being. Recognizing the signs of sickness allows for prompt intervention, potentially saving your turtle from severe health issues. Here are key indicators to watch for:

Changes in Appetite

A sudden decrease in appetite or complete refusal to eat can be a significant warning sign. Turtles are generally eager feeders, and a noticeable drop in their interest in food often indicates underlying health issues. This could range from environmental stressors, such as improper water temperature or quality, to more serious conditions like gastrointestinal problems or infections. Monitor your turtle's eating habits closely, and if you observe a persistent lack of appetite, consult a veterinarian specializing in reptiles.

Swollen Eyes

Swollen or puffy eyes in Red-Eared Sliders can be alarming. This symptom is commonly associated with a vitamin A deficiency, which is critical for maintaining healthy tissues and immune function. Swollen eyes may also signal an infection, either bacterial or fungal. In addition to swelling, other symptoms like redness, discharge, or difficulty opening the eyes are important to note. Addressing dietary deficiencies and seeking veterinary care for potential infections can prevent long-term damage and improve your turtle's overall health.

Lethargy

Turtles are typically active, especially during feeding times and when basking. If your Red-Eared Slider becomes unusually lethargic, it may be feeling unwell. Lethargy can result from a variety of causes, including poor water quality, inadequate basking conditions, or illness. Common illnesses that cause lethargy include respiratory infections, shell infections, or parasitic infestations. Ensuring optimal living conditions and consulting a veterinarian for persistent lethargy is essential to rule out serious health issues.

Abnormal Swimming

Observing your turtle's swimming behavior can provide insights into its health.

Difficulty swimming, swimming in circles, or floating unevenly are red flags. These symptoms often indicate respiratory infections, which are common in aquatic turtles. Other possible causes include internal parasites, neurological issues, or injuries. Respiratory infections can lead to more severe complications if not treated promptly, so it's vital to seek veterinary care if your turtle exhibits abnormal swimming behavior.

Discharge

Any unusual discharge from the nose, mouth, or eyes should be taken seriously. Nasal discharge, often accompanied by sneezing or wheezing, is a classic symptom of respiratory infections. Mouth discharge can indicate oral infections or stomatitis, while eye discharge might suggest conjunctivitis or other eye-related conditions. These signs of discharge can also point to systemic infections that require immediate attention. Regular health check-ups and maintaining a clean and stress-free environment can help prevent these issues.

Preventative Care And Regular Check-Ups

Ensuring the health and well-being of your Red-Eared Slider involves diligent preventative care and routine veterinary check-ups. By focusing on key aspects such as diet, habitat cleanliness, proper lighting, and regular observation, you can significantly enhance your turtle's quality of life and longevity.

Proper Diet: A balanced diet is fundamental to your Red-Eared Slider's health. Their diet should include a mix of vegetables, turtle pellets, and occasional protein sources like insects or small fish. Leafy greens, such as kale and dandelion, are excellent vegetable choices, while commercial turtle pellets ensure they receive essential nutrients. Protein sources, provided sparingly, contribute to their dietary needs without overloading them with fat. It's crucial to ensure they get sufficient vitamin A, which is vital for eye health and immune function, and calcium, which is necessary for strong shell and bone development. A varied diet not only meets their nutritional needs but also keeps them interested in their food.

Clean Habitat: Maintaining a clean habitat is essential to prevent infections and ensure a healthy living environment. Regularly clean their tank, removing uneaten food and waste, and ensure the filter is functioning correctly to keep the water clean and free from harmful bacteria. The water quality in their tank is paramount, as poor conditions can lead to shell rot, respiratory infections, and other health issues. Weekly partial water changes and monthly full cleanings help maintain an optimal environment.

UVB Lighting: Proper UVB lighting is critical for Red-Eared Sliders as it aids in the synthesis of vitamin D3, which is essential for calcium absorption. Without adequate UVB exposure, turtles can develop metabolic bone disease, leading to weak bones and shell deformities. Ensure that your turtle's habitat includes a UVB light source, positioned correctly, and replaced every six to twelve months, as UVB bulbs lose their effectiveness over time.

Regular Vet Visits: Routine veterinary visits are crucial for monitoring your turtle's health. Schedule check-ups at least once a year with a vet who specializes in reptiles. These visits allow for early detection of potential health issues, such as parasites, nutritional deficiencies, or respiratory problems. A professional can provide valuable advice on diet, habitat management, and overall care, tailored to your specific turtle's needs.

Observation: Regularly observe your turtle's behavior and physical condition. Notice changes in eating habits, activity levels, and physical appearance. Early detection of abnormalities, such as lethargy, swollen eyes, or discolored shell spots, can lead to prompt treatment and prevent more serious health issues. Being attentive to your turtle's daily routine helps you catch potential problems early and seek appropriate care.

Handling And Stress Reduction

Handling Red-Eared Sliders with care and reducing their stress is crucial for their overall well-being. Here are some comprehensive tips to ensure their health and happiness.

Limit Handling: Red-Eared Sliders are not particularly fond of being handled. It's best to limit handling to essential occasions, such as during tank cleaning or health checks. Frequent handling can cause stress and discomfort, leading to potential health issues.

Gentle Handling: When handling your turtle, always be gentle. Support their body properly, making sure to hold them securely without squeezing. Avoid quick, sudden movements, as these can startle the turtle and increase stress levels. Handle them close to the ground to prevent injury in case they manage to squirm out of your hands.

Stress-Free Environment: Creating a stress-free environment is vital. Ensure their habitat includes hiding spots where they can retreat and feel safe. This helps them manage stress and provides a sense of security. Incorporate a basking area with proper lighting and temperature regulation to mimic their natural environment. Additionally, avoid placing the tank in high-traffic areas of your home. Constant noise and movement can be very stressful for Red-Eared Sliders.

Consistency: Consistency in their daily routine is key. Turtles thrive on a predictable schedule. Feed them at the same times each day, and maintain a consistent environment regarding temperature, lighting, and humidity levels. This regularity helps reduce stress and promotes a sense of stability.

Minimize Changes: Sudden changes in their environment can be very stressful for Red-Eared Sliders. Avoid introducing new tank mates abruptly or making significant alterations to their habitat layout without a gradual transition. If changes are necessary, implement them slowly to allow the turtle to adjust without becoming overwhelmed. Gradual changes can include slowly moving items within the tank or introducing new elements one at a time.

Regular Health Checks: Perform regular health checks to monitor for signs of stress or illness. Look for changes in behavior, appetite, or physical condition.

Early detection of potential issues can help prevent serious health problems. If you notice anything concerning, consult a veterinarian with experience in reptile care.

Interactive Time: While handling should be limited, spending time near the tank and observing your turtle can be beneficial. This allows the turtle to become accustomed to your presence without the stress of physical handling. Use this time to monitor their behavior and ensure they are active and healthy.

CHAPTER FIVE

BREEDING AND REPRODUCTION

Mating Behavior

Red-eared sliders exhibit fascinating mating behaviors, particularly during the spring when temperatures rise and mating season commences. This period marks increased activity among male sliders as they engage in courtship rituals to attract females. One of the most distinctive behaviors is the courtship dance performed by males. They actively swim in front of females, employing a unique display involving the vibration of their long claws against the sides of the female's head and neck. This fluttering motion serves to capture the female's attention and stimulate her interest in potential mating.

If a female is receptive to the male's advances, she will permit him to mount her, typically engaging in mating underwater. This process is deliberate and can extend over several hours, during which the male internally fertilizes the female's eggs. However, not all courtship attempts are successful, as females may reject advances for various reasons. Sometimes, a female may not yet be ready to mate, or she might simply not be interested in that particular male at that time.

The courtship dance and subsequent mating display of red-eared sliders are crucial aspects of their reproductive behavior. These behaviors ensure the continuation of their species, allowing for genetic diversity and adaptation within their natural habitats. As aquatic turtles, red-eared sliders rely heavily on environmental cues, such as water temperature changes, to signal the onset of mating season. This synchronization ensures that their reproductive efforts align with optimal conditions for offspring survival.

Male sliders invest significant energy and effort in their courtship displays, showcasing their fitness and genetic quality to potential mates. The fluttering of claws against the female's head and neck is not merely a display of vigor but also a tactile communication that likely conveys information about the male's health and reproductive potential. This behavior underscores the evolutionary adaptations that have shaped the mating strategies of red-eared sliders over time, enhancing their chances of successful reproduction in dynamic aquatic environments.

Nesting And Egg-Laying

After the red-eared slider mates, the female embarks on a crucial journey: preparing to lay her eggs. This process begins with a quest for the perfect nesting site. Females meticulously seek out soft, sandy, or loamy soil that provides an ideal environment for nesting. Typically, they choose locations in close proximity to water yet strategically above the flood line to safeguard the nest from potential submersion.

Once a suitable site is identified, the female red-eared slider employs her hind legs to diligently dig a hole. This nest, carefully crafted, can reach several inches in depth, ensuring a secure haven for the forthcoming eggs. When the nest is sufficiently excavated, the female proceeds to lay her clutch of eggs. The number of eggs in each clutch can vary, generally ranging from 10 to 30, influenced by factors such as the female's size and overall health.

After depositing the eggs, a significant moment of maternal instinct unfolds: the female meticulously covers the nest with soil. This protective act serves to shield the eggs from predators and the elements, fostering a safe incubation environment crucial for their development. With her task complete, the female red-eared slider then returns to the water, leaving the buried eggs to embark on their natural journey of incubation.

This process of nesting and egg-laying is not only a testament to the red-eared slider's reproductive cycle but also underscores the species' adaptability and survival strategies. By carefully selecting and preparing nesting sites, females ensure the best possible conditions for their offspring's early development. The act of covering the nest with soil is a critical defense mechanism against potential threats, showcasing the instinctual behavior ingrained in these turtles over generations.

Throughout this process, environmental factors play a pivotal role. The proximity to water ensures easy access for the female slider to navigate between nesting and aquatic habitats, essential for her own well-being and survival post-laying. Meanwhile, the careful choice of soil composition and location underscores the red-eared slider's evolutionary adaptations to terrestrial environments, where the balance between safety and accessibility for future generations is delicately maintained.

Incubation Of Eggs

During the incubation phase of red-eared slider eggs, maintaining precise environmental conditions is crucial for the healthy development of the embryos. These turtles exhibit temperature-dependent sex determination, where the temperature at which the eggs are incubated determines the sex of the hatchlings. Generally, warmer temperatures tend to produce more female hatchlings, while cooler temperatures favor the development of males. The optimal range for incubation is typically between 82°F and 86°F (28°C to 30°C).

In the wild, red-eared slider nests naturally provide suitable conditions of temperature and humidity for egg development. However, when replicating this process in captivity, caretakers must ensure these conditions are carefully monitored and controlled. This is particularly important to prevent the eggs from drying out, as adequate humidity is essential for their survival.

The incubation period for red-eared slider eggs lasts approximately 60 to 90 days, during which maintaining a consistently humid environment is crucial. Humidity levels help prevent the eggs from desiccating and promote proper embryonic development. In captivity, achieving these conditions often involves using specialized reptile egg incubators. These devices are designed to regulate temperature and humidity precisely, mimicking the natural nest environment.

Effective management of the incubation environment involves several key practices. Firstly, the temperature should be monitored closely to ensure it remains within the optimal range throughout the entire incubation period. Fluctuations outside this range can lead to developmental abnormalities or even mortality of the embryos. Secondly, maintaining humidity levels of around 80% to 90% is critical. This high humidity prevents the eggs' shells from drying out, which could otherwise impede the embryos' growth and viability.

Caregivers may use various methods to monitor and adjust these parameters as needed. Some incubators feature digital controls that allow precise adjustment of temperature and humidity settings. Additionally, regular monitoring with a reliable thermometer and hygrometer helps ensure conditions remain stable and suitable for the eggs' development.

Throughout the incubation period, caretakers should also practice careful handling of the eggs to avoid any unnecessary disturbances that could potentially impact their viability. Turning the eggs periodically can help prevent the embryos from sticking to the inside of the shell, ensuring proper development.

Hatchling Care

When the incubation period concludes, the anticipation of new life begins as hatchlings slowly emerge from their eggs. This process can span from several hours to a few days, with hatchlings utilizing a specialized egg tooth to break free from their shells. Unlike many other species, once hatched, the young turtles are left to fend for themselves as their mother does not return to provide care.

In their natural habitat, hatchlings instinctively navigate towards water shortly after emerging from their nests. This stage is fraught with peril, as they become easy targets for various predators like birds, fish, and mammals. Creating a safe environment with ample hiding spots is crucial for their survival during this vulnerable period.

In captivity, ensuring the well-being of hatchlings involves replicating their natural habitat within a controlled setting. This includes setting up a tank with clean, shallow water, a designated basking area warmed by a heat lamp, and the provision of UVB lighting essential for synthesizing vitamin D3, vital for their shell and bone development.

A balanced diet rich in protein is essential for the rapid growth of hatchlings. Offer a diverse array of foods such as small insects, specialized commercial turtle pellets, and finely chopped vegetables. This variety ensures they receive the necessary nutrients for healthy development.

Maintaining a clean environment is paramount, as hatchlings are more susceptible to infections and diseases due to their still-developing immune systems. Regularly monitor water quality and cleanliness to prevent health issues.

To foster optimal growth, provide a habitat that promotes both physical and mental stimulation. Incorporate objects for climbing, hiding, and exploring to encourage natural behaviors and alleviate stress.

CHAPTER SIX

INTERACTION AND ENRICHMENT

Handling Techniques

Handling red-eared sliders requires careful consideration of both their physical and psychological needs. These turtles benefit from proper handling techniques that prioritize their comfort and security. When picking up a red-eared slider, it's important to support their body adequately to prevent any stress or injury. Supporting them under the shell and ensuring a firm but gentle grip helps them feel secure.

Excessive handling should be avoided as it can lead to stress and potentially defensive behaviors such as biting or scratching. It's recommended to limit handling to essential tasks like health checks or tank maintenance. Before and after handling, it's crucial to wash hands thoroughly to prevent the transfer of any harmful pathogens to the turtle.

Regular, gentle handling can help red-eared sliders acclimate to human interaction over time. This can make routine tasks easier and less stressful for both the turtle and the caretaker. However, it's essential to be observant of their body language during handling sessions. Signs of stress in red-eared sliders include retreating into their shells, hissing, or excessive struggling. If these behaviors are observed, it's best to give the turtle space and try handling them again at another time.

Respecting the turtle's boundaries is key to building trust and ensuring their well-being. Providing retreat spaces within their habitat—such as hiding spots or plants—

allows them to feel safe and secure when they need to retreat from interactions. This contributes to their overall comfort and reduces stress levels.

Enrichment Activities

Enrichment activities play a vital role in the well-being of red-eared sliders, ensuring they remain mentally stimulated and physically active. These activities are designed to replicate natural behaviors and provide opportunities for exercise and exploration. By incorporating simple yet effective strategies, caretakers can enhance the overall health and happiness of these beloved turtles.

One of the fundamental enrichment strategies involves diversifying their environment with various surfaces to explore. Rocks, logs, and different textures simulate their natural habitat and encourage behaviors like climbing and basking. These activities not only keep them physically active but also fulfill their innate need for exploration and interaction with their surroundings.

Introducing floating objects or toys further enriches their environment by stimulating curiosity and providing mental stimulation. Objects that move or can be manipulated encourage turtles to investigate and engage in playful behaviors, promoting both physical exercise and mental agility.

Feeding time offers another opportunity for enrichment. By varying the types of food offered—such as leafy greens, vegetables, and occasional proteins—and using food puzzles, caretakers can encourage natural foraging behaviors. Food puzzles, where treats are hidden within a container or submerged in water, require problem-solving skills and provide mental stimulation during mealtime.

Creating a foraging box is another effective enrichment technique. This involves setting up a container with a substrate where food items are hidden. This setup encourages turtles to use their sense of smell and sight to locate food, mimicking their natural foraging instincts. Foraging boxes not only engage their senses but also promote physical activity as they dig and explore to uncover their meals.

Enrichment activities should be varied and regularly rotated to maintain interest and challenge the turtles mentally and physically. Caretakers should observe their red-eared sliders to gauge their preferences and adjust enrichment strategies accordingly. Each turtle may respond differently to various activities, so it's essential to tailor enrichment to individual preferences and behaviors.

Social Interaction With Other Turtles

Red-eared sliders, though typically solitary by nature, can engage in limited social interaction with compatible tankmates, which can be beneficial under controlled conditions. When introducing new turtles to an existing setup, it is essential to first quarantine them to prevent the potential spread of diseases. This precautionary step helps ensure the health and safety of all turtles involved.

Monitoring their interactions closely is crucial during the introduction phase. Signs of aggression, such as biting, chasing, or shell bashing, should be carefully observed. These behaviors indicate potential issues that need prompt attention to prevent injuries or stress among the turtles.

Creating a suitable environment is key to facilitating harmonious social interactions. Adequate space within the tank is essential to reduce competition and allow each turtle to establish its territory comfortably. Providing multiple hiding spots and visual barriers further aids in minimizing direct confrontations and territorial disputes.

If aggression persists despite these measures, it may be necessary to separate the turtles temporarily. During this time, adjustments to the tank setup can be made to alleviate stress factors contributing to the aggression. This could involve repositioning hiding spots, rearranging tank decorations, or even providing additional basking areas to reduce competition for resources.

Reintroducing separated turtles should be approached cautiously. Gradual reintroduction, under continued monitoring, allows turtles to re-establish social hierarchies and potentially develop more amicable relationships. Ensuring each turtle has access to essential resources—such as basking spots, food, and hiding places—fosters a balanced environment that supports social interactions without unnecessary conflict.

Regular observation and proactive management are essential aspects of maintaining a peaceful turtle community. Understanding the individual behaviors and preferences of each turtle helps in creating an environment where they can coexist harmoniously. Additionally, maintaining good water quality and hygiene practices further supports their overall health and reduces stress levels, which can contribute to behavioral issues.

Environmental Enrichment

Environmental enrichment is crucial for ensuring the well-being of tortoises, as it aims to replicate their natural habitat as closely as possible within a captive setting. This involves meticulously designing their enclosure to meet their physiological and behavioral needs.

A key element of environmental enrichment is providing a suitable basking area equipped with a heat lamp. This setup allows tortoises to regulate their body temperature effectively, which is vital for their overall health and metabolic processes. Additionally, UVB lighting is essential as it supports their calcium metabolism, crucial for shell and bone health.

Integrating vegetation into the enclosure, whether live or artificial, serves multiple purposes. Not only does it enhance the aesthetic appeal of the habitat, but it also provides essential hiding spots and opportunities for grazing. This vegetation mimics their natural foraging behavior, promoting mental stimulation and physical activity.

The size of the enclosure is critical; it should be spacious enough to accommodate the tortoise's growth and allow for ample movement. Clean, filtered water should always be available to maintain optimal hydration and water quality.

To prevent monotony and encourage natural behaviors, it's beneficial to regularly alter the layout of the enclosure. This variation stimulates the tortoise's curiosity, prompting exploration and preventing boredom. Observing their behavior closely allows caretakers to fine-tune enrichment strategies based on individual preferences and responses.

Monitoring the tortoise's overall health and well-being is paramount. Adjustments to enrichment activities should be made based on their behavior and interaction with the environment. This proactive approach ensures that the tortoise remains healthy, active, and engaged in their habitat.

CHAPTER SEVEN

LIFESPAN AND AGING

Red-eared sliders are renowned for their remarkably long lifespans among pet turtles, often enduring for several decades when provided with proper care. This longevity underscores the importance of understanding their lifespan and aging processes to ensure optimal care throughout their lives.

Red-eared sliders (Trachemys scripta elegans) typically live between 20 to 40 years in captivity, though some have been known to exceed 50 years with exceptional care. Their lifespan is influenced by various factors, including diet, habitat conditions, and veterinary care. Providing a balanced diet rich in leafy greens, vegetables, and occasional proteins such as insects or commercial turtle pellets supports their health and longevity.

As red-eared sliders age, they undergo physical changes that require attention. They may experience shell anomalies, such as pyramiding or shell rot, which can be managed with proper nutrition, UVB lighting, and maintaining a clean habitat. Regular veterinary check-ups are essential to detect and treat age-related ailments early.

Behaviorally, older red-eared sliders may become less active and spend more time basking. Adjusting their habitat to accommodate their changing needs, such as providing easy access to basking spots and ensuring water quality remains high, supports their well-being.

Understanding the aging process of red-eared sliders empowers keepers to provide proactive care, enhancing their quality of life as they mature. By monitoring their health, diet, and environment closely, turtle enthusiasts can foster companionship with these long-lived reptiles for decades to come.

Life Expectancy Of Red-Eared Sliders

The red-eared slider (Trachemys scripta elegans) is renowned for its impressive longevity, often thriving in captivity for two to four decades, and occasionally surpassing these expectations with exceptional care. Understanding the factors that influence their lifespan can significantly contribute to their well-being and longevity.

In captivity, red-eared sliders typically live between 20 to 40 years. However, instances of individuals exceeding these age ranges are not uncommon, demonstrating the potential for extended lifespans under optimal conditions. Various factors play pivotal roles in determining their longevity, including genetic predispositions, diet, habitat quality, and overall health maintenance.

Genetics lay the foundation for an individual slider's potential lifespan. While some turtles may inherently possess genes conducive to longevity, others may be more susceptible to health issues that can affect their lifespan. This underscores the importance of selecting healthy specimens from reputable sources when acquiring red-eared sliders.

Dietary habits significantly impact the health and longevity of red-eared sliders. A balanced diet is crucial, typically consisting of commercial turtle pellets supplemented with fresh vegetables and occasional protein sources like insects or small fish. Proper nutrition not only supports growth and vitality but also helps prevent obesity and related health complications that can shorten their lifespan.

The quality of their habitat is another critical determinant of lifespan. Red-eared sliders require an appropriate enclosure that meets their spatial and environmental needs. This includes a spacious aquatic area with clean, filtered water and a dry basking area where they can thermoregulate effectively. Proper water quality maintenance and adequate UVB lighting are essential for their overall health and immune function, contributing to a longer, healthier life.

Regular veterinary care and health monitoring are essential aspects of maintaining a red-eared slider's longevity. Routine check-ups can help detect and address potential health issues early, ensuring timely intervention and treatment. This proactive approach, coupled with attentive daily care, such as monitoring behavior, appetite, and shell condition, can significantly enhance their lifespan.

Environmental factors, such as temperature and humidity levels, also influence their health and longevity. Maintaining stable environmental conditions within recommended ranges helps prevent stress-related illnesses and supports their physiological functions.

Signs Of Aging In Red-Eared Sliders

As red-eared sliders advance in age, there are several discernible signs that indicate they are entering their senior years. These signs encompass both physical and behavioral changes, offering caretakers insights into the evolving needs of these beloved turtles.

Firstly, one of the most noticeable indicators of aging in red-eared sliders is the condition of their shell. Over time, the shells of older turtles may exhibit signs of wear and tear. This could manifest as scutes becoming rough or flaky, potentially showing areas where the shell has lost its smooth texture and resilience. Careful observation during regular shell inspections can help caretakers detect these changes early on.

Behavioral shifts also accompany the aging process in red-eared sliders. Older turtles tend to display decreased activity levels compared to their younger counterparts.

While younger sliders may exhibit more energetic behaviors such as swimming or exploring their habitat, seniors often prefer spending extended periods basking under their heat lamp or resting on their basking platforms. This reduced activity is a natural part of aging and should be supported with appropriate basking areas and environmental conditions that facilitate comfort and warmth.

Changes in appetite are another common feature as red-eared sliders age. Senior turtles may demonstrate variations in their eating habits, which can range from a decreased overall appetite to becoming more selective about their food choices. Careful monitoring of their feeding patterns and dietary preferences can help ensure they receive adequate nutrition tailored to their evolving needs.

Moreover, aging red-eared sliders are more prone to health issues than their younger counterparts. Respiratory infections and shell infections are particularly prevalent among older turtles. These health challenges can arise due to a combination of factors including a weakened immune system and the cumulative effects of environmental stressors over the years. Regular veterinary check-ups and proactive health management, such as maintaining clean water conditions and providing a balanced diet, are crucial in mitigating these risks and promoting the longevity and well-being of senior red-eared sliders.

Special Care For Older Turtles

Providing optimal care for aging red-eared sliders requires attentive consideration across various aspects of their well-being.

As turtles age, their dietary needs evolve to align with changes in metabolism and activity levels. It becomes crucial to adjust their diet accordingly, ensuring a balance of nutrients while incorporating adequate calcium and vitamin supplements to support bone health and overall vitality.

Temperature regulation becomes increasingly important for older sliders. Monitoring basking temperatures closely helps maintain their digestive processes and supports immune function. This attention to thermal comfort aids in keeping their metabolic activities optimal, crucial for their longevity and well-being.

Regular veterinary check-ups are essential for older red-eared sliders. These appointments allow for early detection and management of age-related health issues, ensuring timely intervention and maintaining their quality of life. Veterinarians can assess factors such as shell health, organ function, and overall mobility, providing tailored care plans as needed.

Environmental enrichment plays a pivotal role in enhancing the lives of older turtles. Introducing ramps, platforms, and easy access to basking spots within their habitat promotes physical activity and supports mobility. These additions not only encourage natural behaviors but also help prevent issues associated with limited movement, such as joint stiffness or muscle atrophy.

Ensuring a comfortable and enriched environment for aging red-eared sliders involves thoughtful adjustments and regular monitoring. By addressing their dietary, thermal, veterinary, and environmental needs, caretakers can significantly enhance their turtles' quality of life in their later years. Each aspect of care contributes synergistically to promoting longevity and overall well-being, reflecting a commitment to providing compassionate and effective support for these beloved reptilian companions as they age gracefully.

End-Of-Life Care

In the final stages of a red-eared slider's life, caregivers play a crucial role in ensuring their beloved turtle experiences comfort and dignity. As these reptiles age, focusing on their well-being becomes paramount, guided by principles of compassionate care.

Firstly, creating a comfortable environment is essential. This involves providing a quiet and stress-free space where the turtle can feel secure. Maintaining optimal water quality and stable temperatures are key aspects, as changes in these factors can significantly impact the turtle's health and comfort. Ensuring the habitat is clean and well-maintained helps mitigate any additional stress during this sensitive time.

Pain management is another vital consideration. Consulting with a qualified veterinarian to assess and manage any pain or discomfort the turtle may be experiencing is crucial. Veterinarians can recommend appropriate medications or treatments tailored to the turtle's specific needs, ensuring they remain as comfortable as possible.

While reptiles may not display emotions in the same way as mammals, consistent care and attention can provide a sense of security and comfort. This includes maintaining regular feeding schedules, monitoring their behavior for any changes, and providing gentle interaction when appropriate. These actions can help alleviate anxiety and promote a sense of well-being for the turtle during its final stages of life.

Preparing emotionally for the end of a turtle's life is equally important for caregivers. Recognizing the signs of decline, such as decreased activity, loss of appetite, or changes in appearance, can help caregivers anticipate and respond to their turtle's needs effectively. Understanding when humane euthanasia might be necessary is a difficult yet critical decision. Consulting with a veterinarian can provide guidance on assessing quality

of life and making decisions that prioritize
the turtle's comfort and dignity.

THE END